THIS CANDLEWICK BOOK BELONGS TO:

____

____

____

Birrarung Wilam

A Story from Aboriginal Australia

AUNTY JOY MURPHY & ANDREW KELLY
illustrated by LISA KENNEDY

CANDLEWICK PRESS

“Me no leave it,
Yarra, my country.
There’s no mountains
for me on the Murray.”

WILLIAM BARAK, 1874
WURUNDJERI NGURUNGAETA

As ngua rises,
turning clouds over the distant city red,
Bunjil soars over mountain ash,
flying higher and higher as the wind warms.

Below, Birrarung begins its long
winding path down to palem warreen.

Deep in the yerin,
wallert comes home
to sleep in a bark-lined nest
inside a hollow tree.
Parnmin falls on djerang,
flows down wirrip, and soaks
into yeameneen beek.

As more rain falls, baan begins
to flow over yeameneen beek
and gathers into yaluk.
Nearby, boroin perches on kombadick,
anxiously calling to her mate
in his bright-blue breeding colors.
He flits from frond to frond, chasing insects.
Soon yaluk joins with yaluk
and becomes Birrarung.

Yanggai fly down the valley
with great slow flapping wingbeats,
searching for the pines
planted where Birrarung
has been dammed.
Pine cones are rich with seeds.

Where Birrarung begins to run through farmland,
marram, resting on soft forepaws,
neatly clips buath.
From her pouch, murrum looks out.

Hidden behind tangled roots in
the bank of Birrarung,
dulai-wurrung lies in her burrow,
curled around her newly hatched babies.

Waa flies along Birrarung
with his brothers,
making his slow high call,
drawing out the last note
so everyone can hear.

From her long burrow in the bank
of Birrarung, warin comes out
to eat. In her pouch is her young one.
Her pouch opens backward,
so she doesn't flick in dirt when she digs.

Tadjerri sleeps snuggled in a nesting box,
fixed to a garrang. He dreams of
gliding from tree to tree, and
of sweet nectar and tasty insects.

Near the city, bathmu shares a nest
with eight little ducklings.

In evening light, boggon scurries along
the edge of Birrarung looking for dinner,
maybe a tasty fish or two.
Drips fall from his waterproof fur.
He flicks his thick white-tipped tail.

As ngua sets,
wadjil floats on the
surface, ready to dive.
She watches carefully for
the silvery flicker of a
school of anchovies
she can surprise with
a scoop of her huge bill.
Sharp-eyed Bunjil soars
overhead, watching
everything spread out
beneath him. Fresh water,
which began its journey
as parnmin falling on
djerang, mixes into
palem warreen.
Birrarung is wilam
to many.

GLOSSARY

The Woiwurrung language does not translate directly into English.

ngua (NOO-ah): sun

Bunjil (BAHN-jool): wedge-tailed eagle. Bunjil is the creator spirit of the Wurundjeri people.

Birrarung (BEER-ah-rung): Woiwurrung word for river of mists, often called the Yarra

palem warreen (pah-LEM wah-REEN): salt water; bay

yerin (YEE-rin): bush

wallert (WOLL-ert): possum. The Leadbeater's possum lives in forests of the Central Highlands, where Birrarung (the Yarra River) begins to flow.

parnmin (PAHN-meen): rain

djerang (JEE-rang): leaves

wirrip (WEER-up): trunk

yeameneen beek (YEE-meh-neen beek): earth

wilam: home

baan (bahn): water

yeameneen beek (YEE-meh-neen beek): earth

yaluk (YAH-luk): creek

boroin (BOH-roin): superb fairy-wren

kombadick (KOM-bah-dik): tree fern

Birrarung (BEER-ah-rung): Yarra River

yanggai (YANG-guy): black cockatoo; yellow-tailed black cockatoo

Birrarung (BEER-ah-rung): Yarra River

Birrarung (BEER-ah-rung): Yarra River

marram (MA-rum): gray kangaroo

buath (BOO-ath): grass

murrum (MAH-rum): joey (baby kangaroo)

Birrarung (BEER-ah-rung): Yarra River

dulai-wurrung (DOO-lay-wuh-RUNG): platypus

waa (waah): raven, sometimes called crow

Birrarung (BEER-ah-rung): Yarra River

Birrarung (BEER-ah-rung): Yarra River

warin (WAR-ren): wombat

tadjerri (tah-DJEE-ree): sugar glider possum

garrang (GA-rang): eucalyptus tree

bathmu (BATH-moo): duck; wood duck

boggon (BOH-gon): water rat, sometimes called rakali

Birrarung (BEER-ah-rung): Yarra River

ngua (NOO-ah): sun

wadjil (WAH-djool): pelican

bunjil (BAHN-jool): wedge-tailed eagle

parnmin (PAHN-meen): rain

djerang (JEER-ang): leaves

palem warreen (pah-LEM wah-REEN): salt water; bay

Birrarung (BEER-ah-rung): Yarra River

wilam (WIL-um): home

JOY MURPHY WANDIN AO
is the Senior Aboriginal Elder of the Wurundjeri people of Melbourne and the surrounding area. We show respect for her and other Elders by calling them Aunty or Uncle.

Aunty Joy is a storyteller and a writer and is passionate about using story to bring people together and as a conduit for understanding Aboriginal culture.

Aunty Joy is a daughter of James and Olive Wandin, who gave her a lifetime of learning.

ANDREW KELLY
grew up along the Birrarung in South Yarra. He is passionate about the Birrarung (Yarra) and is the Yarra Riverkeeper. It is the role of the Riverkeeper to speak for the Yarra on behalf of the community. He thanks Aunty Joy Murphy and Lisa Kennedy for the opportunity to work with them on this book.

LISA KENNEDY
is a descendant of the Trawlwoolway people on the northeast coast of Tasmania. She was born in Melbourne and as a child lived close to the Maribyrnong River. Here she experienced the gradual restoration of the natural river environment alongside cultural regeneration and reclamation. Through sense of place, she feels connected to the Wurundjeri country and all that entails—the water, the land, the animals, and the ancestors. The experience of loss and reclamation is embedded in her work.

First U.S. paperback edition 2022
First published by Walker Books Australia 2019

Library of Congress Catalog Card Number 2020910715
ISBN 978-1-5362-0942-6 (hardback)
ISBN 978-1-5362-2774-1 (paperback)

22 23 24 25 26 27 CCP
1 2 3 4 5 6 7 8 9 10

Printed in Shenzhen, Guangdong, China

This book was typeset in Maiandra Condensed.
The illustrations were done in acrylic.

Candlewick Press
99 Dover Street
Somerville, Massachusetts 02144

visit us at www.candlewick.com

Peter, thank you for your love
and always standing tall and strong beside me. xo
Sophie Elizabeth, you are a GEM.
And buckets of love to all our kids,
grandkids, and great-grandkids. xo
Meme McDonald (Waderbirds —
Odyssey of the Wetlands), my dearest friend. xo
J. M.

To Trishie,
for giving me my love of books.
A. K.

In loving memory of my sister Maria.
Your poems and pictures were my
first inspiration.
And to my children, who have
inherited the Healing.
L. K.